Penguin Books

STRICTLY PRIVATE

an anthology of poetry
chosen by Roger McGough

Keep out of this book if you like dissecting dusty old verse, for this is a collection of today's poetry that is fresh and very much alive! Roger McGough has gathered an exciting anthology of contemporary poems that will speak to every young reader. Contributors include Adrian Mitchell, Ted Hughes, Ivor Cutler, Charles Causley, and Roger McGough himself.

Within these strictly guarded pages all sorts of poems lie waiting to be discovered, to be enjoyed, to question the usual answers and to dream the special dreams. Here are poems about life in towns and in the country-side, about games, school and leaving school, animals, likes and hates, and there are poems to laugh at and poems of love and emotion:

> *Poems to be looked at in silence*
> *Poems to be sung and shouted*
> *Poems that tickle*
> *Poems that trip you up as you're going past*
> *Poems that . . .*

Roger McGough was born in Liverpool in 1937, the son of a doctor. He received a BA degree in French and Geography from the University of Hull and then taught for three years before becoming famous with 'The Scaffold' and as a poet. He has had several volumes of his poems published, as well as plays and sketches, and his poetry readings are immensely popular.

Other books by Roger McGough

IN TIME OF WAR
SO FAR, SO GOOD

for younger readers

AN IMAGINARY MENAGERIE
NAILING THE SHADOW
SKY IN THE PIE

STRICTLY PRIVATE

AN ANTHOLOGY OF POETRY

CHOSEN BY ROGER McGOUGH

illustrated by Graham Dean

PENGUIN BOOKS

STRICTLY PRIVATE
KEEP OFF THE PAGES

PENGUIN BOOKS

Published by the Penguin Group
27 Wrights Lane, London w8 5tz, England
Viking Penguin Inc., 40 West 23rd Street, New York, New York 10010, USA
Penguin Books Australia Ltd, Ringwood, Victoria, Australia
Penguin Books Canada Ltd, 2801 John Street, Markham, Ontario, Canada l3r 1b4
Penguin Books (NZ) Ltd, 182–190 Wairau Road, Auckland 10, New Zealand

Penguin Books Ltd, Registered Offices: Harmondsworth, Middlesex, England

First published in Kestrel Books 1981
Published in Puffin Books 1982
Reprinted in Penguin Books 1988
3 5 7 9 10 8 6 4

Made and printed in Great Britain by
Richard Clay Ltd, Bungay, Suffolk
Set in Monotype Baskerville

Contents

Foreword

Foreword is forearmed, so herewith the poems:
Poems to be looked at in silence
Poems to be sung and shouted
Poems that tickle
Poems that trip you up as you're going past
Poems to tell your mates
Poems so secret you keep them to yourself
Poems not to be seen out alone with
Poems with insights and outsights
Poems that go bump in the night
Poems that . . . (and anyway, what are
you doing messing about in my preface
when you should be over the page
and in amongst the real stuff. Be
off with you. Get

        thee

          hen

            ce)

FIRST DAY AT SCHOOL

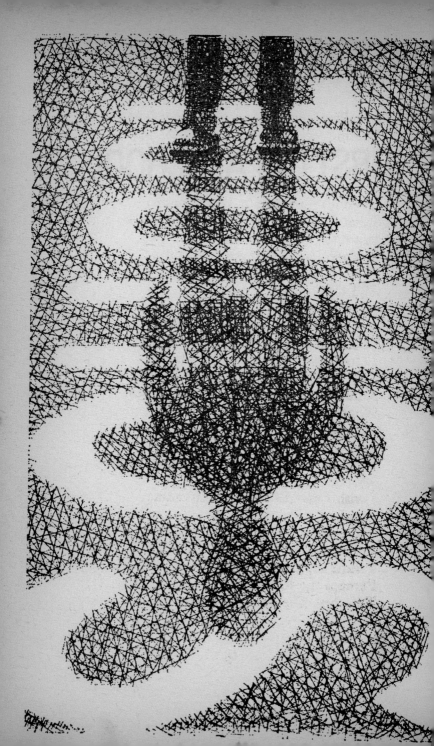

First Day at School

A millionbillionwillion miles from home
Waiting for the bell to go. (To go where?)
Why are they all so big, other children?
So noisy? So much at home they
must have been born in uniform.
Lived all their lives in playgrounds.
Spent the years inventing games
that don't let me in. Games
that are rough, that swallow you up.

And the railings.
All around, the railings.
Are they to keep out wolves and monsters?
Things that carry off and eat children?
Things you don't take sweets from?
Perhaps they're to stop us getting out.
Running away from the lessins. Lessin.
What does a lessin look like?
Sounds small and slimy.
They keep them in glassrooms.
Whole rooms made out of glass. Imagine.

I wish I could remember my name.
Mummy said it would come in useful.
Like wellies. When there's puddles.
Yellowwellies. I wish she was here.
I think my name is sewn on somewhere.
Perhaps the teacher will read it for me.
Tea-cher. The one who makes the tea.

Roger McGough

Schoolpoem 2

One day i went into the school library and
        there were no books. Panic-stricken
i looked for explanations in the eyes
        of a school-tied librarian but
she just stamped a date on my wrist
        and said i was overdue.
Then i spied one little book called
        'HOW TO SPELL'
                but
        i new how to do that already,
    so i sat feeling pretty lonely
as you can imagine in a bookless library,
        in the skeleton of a library,
going over all the names of books i once new:
        WAR AND PEACE
        DANNY THE DORMOUSE
    how nice and neat and safe they were.
    Now all i do is look for answers
        in my blazer pockets but
    they have gone through the holes
        made by yesterday's
            marbles.

Brian McCabe

Dad

The trouble with me is
i take everything for granted
CAMBODIA – 50,000 dead gee whizz pass the
salt.
i take wars for granted
My dad says it's all because i'm younger
than the bomb.
But the trouble with me is
i take the bomb for granted.
He says
i won't bloody well
take it for granted
when it drops on my head.

i take my head for granted.

Brian McCabe

Oh bring back higher standards

Oh bring back higher standards –
the pencil and the cane –
if we want education then we must have some pain.
Oh, bring us back all the gone days
Yes, bring back all the past . . .
let's put them all in rows again – so we can see who's
    last.
Let's label all the good ones
(the ones like you and me)
and make them into prefects – like prefects used to be.
We'll put them on the honours board
. . . as honours ought to be,
and write their names in burnished script –
for all the world to see.
We'll have them back in uniform,
we'll have them doff their caps,
and learn what manners really are
. . . for decent kind of chaps!
. . . So let's label all the good ones,
we'll call them 'A's and 'B's –
and we'll parcel up the useless ones
and call them 'C's and 'D's.
. . . We'll even have an 'E' lot!
. . . an 'F' or 'G' maybe!!
. . . so they can know they're useless,
. . . and not as good as me.

For we've got to have the stupid –
And we've got to have the poor
Because –
        if we don't have them . . .
        well . . . what are prefects for?

Peter Dixon

Arithmetic

I'm 11. And I don't really know
my Two Times Table. Teacher says it's
    disgraceful
But even if I had the time, I feel too tired.
Ron's 5, Samantha's 3, Carole's 18 months,
and then there's Baby. I do what's required.

Mum's working. Dad's away. And so
I dress them, give them breakfast. Mrs Russell
moves in, and I take Ron to school.
Miss Eames calls me an old-fashioned word:
    Dunce.
Doreen Maloney says I'm a fool.

After tea, to the Rec. Pram-pushing's slow
but on fine days it's a good place, full
of larky boys. When 6 shows on the clock
I put the kids to bed. I'm free for once.
At about 7 – Mum's key in the lock.

Gavin Ewart

Common Sense

An agricultural labourer, who has
A wife and four children, receives 20s a week
$\frac{3}{4}$ buys food, and the members of the family
Have three meals a day.
How much is that per person per meal?
     – From Pitman's Common Sense Arithmetic, 1917

A gardener, paid 24s a week, is
Fined $\frac{1}{3}$ if he comes to work late.
At the end of 26 weeks, he receives
£30.5.3. How
Often was he late?
     – From Pitman's Common Sense Arithmetic, 1917

A milk dealer buys milk at 3d a quart. He
Dilutes it with 3% water and sells
124 gallons of the mixture at
4d per quart. How much of his profit is made by
Adulterating the milk?
     – From Pitman's Common Sense Arithmetic, 1917

The table printed below gives the number
Of paupers in the United Kingdom, and
The total cost of poor relief.
Find the average number
Of paupers per ten thousand people.
     – From Pitman's Common Sense Arithmetic, 1917

An army had to march to the relief of
A besieged town, 500 miles away, which
Had telegraphed that it could hold out for 18 days.
The army made forced marches at the rate of 18
Miles a day. Would it be there in time?
     – From Pitman's Common Sense Arithmetic, 1917

Out of an army of 28,000 men,
15% were
Killed, 25% were
Wounded. Calculate
how many men there were left to fight.
     – From Pitman's Common Sense Arithmetic, 1917

These sums are offered to
That host of young people in our Elementary Schools,
   who
Are so ardently desirous of setting
Foot upon the first rung of the
Educational ladder . . .
     – From Pitman's Common Sense Arithmetic, 1917

                                 Alan Brownjohn

The Choosing

We were first equal Mary and I
with the same coloured ribbons in mouse-coloured
  hair,
and with equal shyness
we curtseyed to the lady councillor
for copies of Collins' Children's Classics.
First equal, equally proud.

Best friends too Mary and I
a common bond in being cleverest (equal)
in our small school's small class.
I remember
the competition for top desk
or to read aloud the lesson
at school service.
And my terrible fear
of her superiority at sums.

I remember the housing scheme
Where we both stayed.
The same house, different homes,
where the choices were made.

I don't know exactly why they moved,
but anyway they went.
Something about a three-apartment
and a cheaper rent.
But from the top deck of the high-school bus
I'd glimpse among the others on the corner
Mary's father, mufflered, contrasting strangely
with the elegant greyhounds by his side.

He didn't believe in high-school education,
especially for girls,
or in forking out for uniforms.

Ten years later on a Saturday –
I am coming home from the library –
sitting near me on the bus,
Mary
with a husband who is tall,
curly haired, has eyes
for no one else but Mary.
Her arms are round the full-shaped vase
that is her body.
Oh, you can see where the attraction lies
in Mary's life –
not that I envy her, really.

And I am coming from the library
with my arms full of books.
I think of the prizes that were ours for the taking
and wonder when the choices got made
we don't remember making.

Liz Lochhead

Winter

On Winter mornings in the playground
The boys stand huddled,
Their cold hands doubled
Into trouser pockets.
The air hangs frozen
About the buildings
And the cold is an ache in the blood
And a pain on the tender skin
Beneath finger nails.
The odd shouts
Sound off like struck iron
And the sun
Balances white
Above the boundary wall.
I fumble my bus ticket
Between numb fingers
Into a fag,
Take a drag
And blow white smoke
Into the December air.

Gareth Owen

Street Boy

Just you look at me, man,
Stompin' down the street
My crombie stuffed with biceps
My boots is filled with feet.

Just you hark to me, man,
When they call us out
My head is full of silence
My mouth is full of shout.

Just you watch me move, man,
Steady like a clock
My heart is spaced on blue beat
My soul is stoned on rock.

Just you read my name, man,
Writ for all to see
The walls is red with stories
The streets is filled with me.

                                    Gareth Owen

Dumb Insolence

I'm big for ten years old
Maybe that's why they get at me

Teachers, parents, cops
Always getting at me

When they get at me

I don't hit em
They can do you for that

I don't swear at em
They can do you for that

I stick my hands in my pockets
And stare at them

And while I stare at them
I think about sick

They call it dumb insolence

They don't like it
But they can't do you for it

I've been done before
They say if I get done again

They'll put me in a home
So I do dumb insolence

Adrian Mitchell

The Lesson

A poem that raises the question:
Should there be capital punishment in schools?

Chaos ruled OK in the classroom
as bravely the teacher walked in
the nooligans ignored him
his voice was lost in the din

'The theme for today is violence
and homework will be set
I'm going to teach you a lesson
one that you'll never forget'

He picked on a boy who was shouting
and throttled him then and there
then garotted the girl behind him
(the one with grotty hair)

Then sword in hand he hacked his way
between the chattering rows
'First come, first severed' he declared
'fingers, feet, or toes'

He threw the sword at a latecomer
it struck with deadly aim
then pulling out a shotgun
he continued with his game

The first blast cleared the backrow
(where those who skive hang out)
they collapsed like rubber dinghies
when the plug's pulled out

'Please may I leave the room sir?'
a trembling vandal enquired
'Of course you may' said teacher
put the gun to his temple and fired

The Head popped a head round the doorway
to see why a din was being made
nodded understandingly
then tossed in a grenade

And when the ammo was well spent
with blood on every chair
Silence shuffled forward
with its hands up in the air

The teacher surveyed the carnage
the dying and the dead
He waggled a finger severely
'Now let that be a lesson' he said

Roger McGough

Thug

School began it.
There he felt
the tongue's salt lash
raising its welt

on a child's heart.
Ten years ruled
by violence left him
thoroughly schooled,

nor did he fail
to understand
the blow of the
headmaster's hand.

That hand his hand
round the cosh curled.
What rules the classroom
rocks the world.

Raymond Garlick

'His case is typical'

His case is typical.
On leaving school he showed no tendency to seek
honest employment. I visited him often.
I formed the opinion he wasn't
inherently vicious
however
during his formative years something has snapped.

He thought everyone was against him.
He took a dislike to this Chaplain.
He failed to draw strength from the Bible.

Though the guards showed him nothing but kindness
he made no attempt to lighten their task.
He sulked. He was bitter.
And on the last day when the privilege to choose
a reasonable menu is given to those who must die
he neglected the offer,
he sat saying nothing.

I asked him to listen. I said to him, lad
wait till the cyanide egg hits the acid
then draw a deep breath,
trying to help him in spite of his coldness.
I held out my hand to him.

Next day I had a visit from his mother.
You were only doing your duty, Governor.
You did your best and have a mother's thanks.

Your boy was one of my failures, Ma'am.
How could he think the world was against him
with someone like you at his back?

Christopher Logue

HE'S BEHIND YER

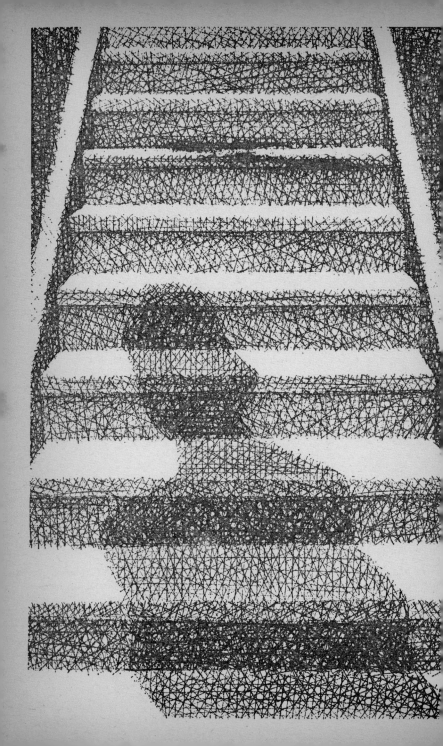

He's Behind Yer

'HE'S BEHIND YER!'
chorused the children
but the warning came too late.

The monster leaped forward
and fastening its teeth into his neck,
tore off the head.

The body fell to the floor
'MORE' cried the children

'MORE'' MORE'

'MORE'

'

M

Roger McGough

What Has Happened to Lulu?

What has happened to Lulu, mother?
  What has happened to Lu?
There's nothing in her bed but an old rag doll
  And by its side a shoe.

Why is her window wide, mother,
  The curtain flapping free,
And only a circle on the dusty shelf
  Where her money-box used to be?

Why do you turn your head, mother,
  And why do the tear-drops fall?
And why do you crumple that note on the fire
  And say it is nothing at all?

I woke to voices late last night,
  I heard an engine roar.
Why do you tell me the things I heard
  Were a dream and nothing more?

I heard somebody cry, mother,
  In anger or in pain,
But now I ask you why, mother,
  You say it was a gust of rain.

Why do you wander about as though
  You don't know what to do?
What has happened to Lulu, mother?
  What has happened to Lu?

Charles Causley

Thinks

you think
it can't last
it should all be over by midnight
or tomorrow lunchtime at the outside

but it goes on
and nobody stoops
to handle the brake

it goes on
and very soon you get to understand
that
perhaps it will last after all
pretty soon you get to saying to yourself

I must do something
about this

so you settle down with a good book
under the arc lamps of reality
you dissect the words
and keep them in vinegar
you take a little love
and you bruise it in your palm
you take a little hope
and boil it in your fear
you laugh a little
cry a little
start to blow your nose
and you think

perhaps a storm would turn off the sun
perhaps we'll all learn to work out the facts

so you put out the flags
as you turn out the lights
and much later

about a lifetime
later

one dark night
in the cold of your bed
you sit up with a start
with a voice in your head

and you say to yourself

I must do something
about this

Miles Gibson

Beware of the Stars

That star
Will blow your hand off

That star
Will scramble your brains and your nerves

That star
Will frizzle your skin off

That star
Will turn everybody yellow and stinking

That star
Will scorch everything dead fumed to its blueprint

That star
Will make the earth melt

That star . . . and so on.

And they surround us. And far into infinity.
These are the armies of the night.
We are totally surrounded.
There is no escape.
Not one of them is good, or friendly, or corruptible.

One chance remains: KEEP ON DIGGING THAT HOLE

KEEP ON DIGGING AWAY AT THAT HOLE

Ted Hughes

Three

Where three fields meet
there's good water –
strong as forge-water
it makes you well.

Dreamed three times
the dream is true
though three times three bells
knell a man
and three times two a woman.

North of here
they'll tie two boats together
that none might be
the third to leave the harbour.

In 1914 in the New Forest
an old woman was not surprised
for all the Spring and Summer
her people counted overhead
the wild swans fly in threes and threes.

Peter Fallon

The Radish

I'm a left wing radish, raw and
red as a thumped nose, body scabbed
where dirt hurt. It was you who set

me down in that regimented
plot where I knew the poverty
of stones, grew up under the superb

stars, and felt waters freeze in my
head. But I survived that waste land
for you to rip me out when I

sprouted messages of a green
spring to come. You raped my family,
tore up the roots, transported us

to this fearful kitchen camp and
dropped me, castrated and scoured, bald
as a cold sun, onto this white plate.

I see you coming, mouth alive
with tortures, itching to screw my
groin in salt, but when I open

my heart and broken lie in the
folded flag of your tongue then will
my whiteness bite, bite finally.

Wes Magee

The Apple's Song

Tap me with your finger,
rub me with your sleeve,
hold me, sniff me, peel me
curling round and round
till I burst out white and cold
from my tight red coat
and tingle in your palm
as if I'd melt and breathe
a living pomander
waiting for the minute
of joy when you lift me
to your mouth and crush me
and in taste and fragrance
I race through your head
in my dizzy dissolve.

I sit in the bowl
in my cool corner
and watch you as you pass
smoothing your apron.
Are you thirsty yet?
My eyes are shining.

Edwin Morgan

Hyena

I am waiting for you.
I have been travelling all morning through the bush
and not eaten.
I am lying at the edge of the bush
on a dusty path that leads from the burnt-out kraal.
I am panting, it is midday, I found no water-hole.
I am very fierce without food and although my eyes
are screwed to slits against the sun
you must believe I am prepared to spring.

What do you think of me?
I have a rough coat like Africa.
I am crafty with dark spots
like the bush-tufted plains of Africa.
I sprawl as a shaggy bundle of gathered energy
like Africa sprawling in its waters.
I trot, I lope, I slaver, I am a ranger.
I hunch my shoulders. I eat the dead.

Do you like my song?
When the moon pours hard and cold on the veldt
I sing, and I am the slave of darkness.
Over the stone walls and the mud walls and the ruined
    places
and the owls, the moonlight falls.
I sniff a broken drum. I bristle. My pelt is silver.
I howl my song to the moon – up it goes.
Would you meet me there in the waste places?

It is said I am a good match
for a dead lion. I put my muzzle
at his golden flanks, and tear. He
is my golden supper, but my tastes are easy.
I have a crowd of fangs, and I use them.
Oh and my tongue – do you like me
when it comes lolling out of my jaw
very long, and I am laughing?
I am not laughing.
But I am not snarling either, only
panting in the sun, showing you
what I grip
carrion with.

I am waiting
for the foot to slide,
for the heart to seize,
for the leaping sinews to go slack,
for the fight to the death to be fought to the death,
for a glazing eye and the rumour of blood.
I am crouching in my dry shadows
till you are ready for me.
My place is to pick you clean
and leave your bones to the wind.

Edwin Morgan

The Fish Are All Sick

The fish are all sick, the great whales dead,
The villages stranded in stone on the coast,
Ornamental, like pearls on the fringe of a coat.
Sea men, who knew what the ocean did,
Turned their low houses away from the surf.
But new men who come to be rural and safe
Add big glass views and begonia beds.
Water keeps to itself.
White lip after lip
Curls to a close on the littered beach.
Something is sicker and blacker than fish.
And closing its grip, and closing its grip.

Anne Stevenson

The Lake

For years there have been no fish in the lake.
People hurrying through the park avoid it
like the plague. Birds steer clear
and the sedge of course has withered.
Trees lean away from it,
and at night it reflects, not the moon,
but the blackness of its own depths.
There are no fish in the lake.
But there is life there. There is life . . .

Underwater pigs glide between reefs of coral debris.
They love it here. They breed and multiply
in sties hollowed out of the mud
and lined with mattresses and bedsprings.
They live on dead fish and rotting things,
drowned pets, plastic and assorted excreta.
Rusty cans they like the best.
Holding them in webbed trotters
their teeth tear easily through the tin,
and poking in a snout, they noisily suck out
the putrid matter within.

There are no fish in the lake.
But there is life there. There is life . . .

For on certain evenings after dark
shoals of pigs surface
and look out at those houses near the park.
Where, in bathrooms,
children feed stale bread to plastic ducks,
and in attics,
toy yachts have long since runaground.

Where, in livingrooms,
anglers dangle their lines on patterned carpets,
and bemoan the fate of the ones that got away.

Down on the lake, piggy eyes glisten.
They have acquired a taste for flesh.
They are licking their lips. Listen . . .

Roger McGough

'*You fit into me*'

you fit into me
like a hook into an eye

a fish hook
an open eye.

Margaret Atwood

Fishermen

the fishermen are patient
their lines settle in clear water
their wide-brimmed hats
will keep off
everything

on the boulevards meantime
carriages come and go
they carry
doctors to quiet basements
and children to circuses
music masters to doleful violins
and lovers to strange ceremonies
of whalebone and gardenias

the fishermen are unimpressed

over clear water
where the rod's end dances
the world is almost
under control

and everything that matters
is just
about to happen

Alasdair Paterson

Goldfish

the scene of the crime
was a goldfish bowl
goldfish were kept
in the bowl at the time:

that was the scene
and that was the crime

Alan Jackson

Nebula

The birds don't believe
we are here, on the road
swooping to die
before a fast car; ignoring us.

A fat pigeon with a damaged
wing strutting from
the sidewalk and under
an enormous green bus

like a rushing forest or an
overclouded sky. I stood
looking at the feathers
and into the excited

eyes of a child, marvelling
at the sound of its death,
still expanding
a thousand years later.

Henry Graham

Along the promenade

Along the promenade
come the mentally-handicapped.
With them is a black-gowned nun.
She watches as they run
along the neat, flagged path.

48

The sand is grey, but clean.
The seagulls play
at the water's edge, with
fingery feet.

The gush of drains is heard.
The stench of waste is almost
indiscernible.

The faces of the children
are moonlike.
They fill the parade.
They are pallid balloons
held in the holy grasp
of a nun.

I
run.

Later, the cherry tree
that had begun to bloom
in my imagination
drops its blossoms
into the chill, May rain.

I see those faces
rising.
And call my son's name
again – and again – and again . . .

Olga Benjamin

A Phantasy

This plump boy, simple, scared of everything
Told me he'd like to live in a cardboard box
With eye holes, ear holes, air holes.

After two years of treatment he had reached the point
Where only one fear remained: drowning.
He had nightmares of being sucked into the waves.

A hundred miles from the sea, walking
To school along a road two miles from any water,
A grain truck passed him on a tight corner,

Spilled its load over him.
The driver said he saw the grain moving
And tried, though injured, to dig down.

There were sounds too. Long bleating cries.
He thought it was a sheep he'd buried.
And the boy died.

John Ashbrook

Slow reader

He can make sculptures
And fabulous machines
Invent games, tell jokes
Give solemn, adult advice
But he is slow to read.
When I take him on my knee
With his *Ladybird* book
He gazes into the air
Sighing and shaking his head
Like an old man
Who knows the mountains
Are impassable.

He toys with words
Letting them grow cold
As gristly meat
Until I relent
And let him wriggle free –
A fish returning
To its element
Or a white-eyed colt
Shying from the bit
As if he sees
That if he takes it
In his mouth
He'll never run
Quite free again.

Vicki Feaver

Strangers and Sweets

everywhere children go in danger
of being accosted and having their love
bribed or harshly demanded from them; not least by
these familiar strangers that lurk in their houses
and claim them as a right.

Dave Calder

Song of the Child

the child ran to the mountain
and he pulled the rocks about
– I'll take you to the cleaners you old mountain
for I'll let the fountain out

the child ran to his daddy
and he pulled his beard about
– I'll knock you off your rocky chair old daddy
for I'm what you're about

the child ran to the holies
and he pulled their spires about
– I'll strip your lead for soldiers you old holies
for your games are all played out

the child ran to the soldiers
and he pulled their guns about
– I'll teach you to play war games you old soldiers
for it's turn and turn about

the child ran to the heavens
and he pulled the stars about
– I'll have you for my bathmat you old heavens
for I've drawn the plug right out

the child ran to the waters
and he pulled the dead about
– I'll wear you when you're broken you old waters
for now I'm coming out

Edwin Morgan

Infant Song

Don't you love my baby, mam,
Lying in his little pram,

Polished all with water clean,
The finest baby ever seen?

Daughter, daughter, if I could
I'd love the baby as I should,

But why the suit of signal red,
The horns that grow out of his head,

Why does he burn with brimstone heat,
Have cloven hooves instead of feet,

Fishing hooks upon each hand,
The keenest tail that's in the land,

Pointed ears and teeth so stark
And eyes that flicker in the dark?

Don't you love my baby, mam?

Dearest, I do not think I can.
I do not, do not think I can.

Charles Causley

Witch Spawn

It's true I knew her Mother burned;
The girl seemed simple, free from guile;
Man is but man: my head was turned.
(A witch she was with her slow, rare smile.)

I have no knowledge of how she charmed,
Some said she fed on serpent's milk;
Yet child or beast she never harmed.
(A witch she was but her skin was silk.)

Small creatures answered to her call
Fearlessly running to her feet,
She lived amongst them: knew them all.
(A witch she was, so warm and sweet.)

Her eyes were neither blue nor grey,
So dark at night; I never did see
What colour they were by light of day.
(A witch she was as she lay with me.)

They say she bore the Devil's brat:
Only I and my mirror can tell
How often the Devil has worn my hat!
(A witch she was but she pleased me well.)

'She'll cast her eye on our men for sure,
And suck their wits!' the women said;
They stoned her windows and broke her door.
(A witch she was with her wild, dark head.)

They dragged her out to the market square
Half mad with fear, her hair close shorn;
The stake stood high and they bound her there.
(A witch she was, of a true witch born.)

She screamed and spat at the rush of flame
As it touched her flesh – and I half turned,
Fearing she might call my name . . .

A witch she was. As such – she burned.

Beth Cross

Kill the Children

On Hallowe'en in Ship Street,
quite close to Benny's bar,
the children lit a bonfire
and the adults parked a car.

Sick minds sing sentimental songs
and speak in dreary prose
and make ingenious home-made bombs –
and this was one of those.

Some say it was the UVF
and some the IRA
blew up that pub on principle
and killed the kids at play.

They didn't mean the children,
it only was the blast;
we call it KILL THE CHILDREN DAY
in bitter old Belfast.

James Simmons

The Identification

So you think its Stephen?
Then I'd best make sure
Be on the safe side as it were.
Ah, theres been a mistake. The hair
you see, its black, now Stephens fair . . .
Whats that? The explosion?
Of course, burnt black. Silly of me.
I should have known. Then lets get on.

The face, is that a face I ask?
that mask of charred wood
blistered, scarred could
that have been a child's face?
The sweater, where intact, looks
in fact all too familiar.
But one must be sure.

The scoutbelt. Yes thats his.
I recognise the studs he hammered in
not a week ago. At the age
when boys get clothes-conscious
now you know. Its almost
certainly Stephen. But one must
be sure. Remove all trace of doubt.
Pull out every splinter of hope.

Pockets. Empty the pockets.
Handkerchief? Could be any schoolboy's.
Dirty enough. Cigarettes?
Oh this can't be Stephen.
I dont allow him to smoke you see.
He wouldn't disobey me. Not his father.
But thats his penknife. Thats his alright.
And thats his key on the keyring
Gran gave him just the other night.
Then this must be him.

I think I know what happened
. . . . . . about the cigarettes
No doubt he was minding them
for one of the older boys.
Yes thats it.
Thats him.
Thats our Stephen.

Roger McGough

Time Child

Dandelion, dandelion,
Dandelion flower,
If I breathe upon thee
Pray tell me the hour.

Little child, little child,
Little child I pray,
Breathe but gently on me
Lest you blow the time away.

Gareth Owen

TIDE AND TIME

Tide and Time

My Aunty Jean
was no mean hortihorologist.
For my fifteenth birthday
she gave me a floral wristwatch.
Wormproof and self-weeding,
its tick was as soft
as a butterfly on tiptoe.

All summer long
I sniffed happily the passing hours.
Until late September
when, forgetting to take it off
before bathing at New Brighton,
the tide washed time away.

Roger McGough

The Round Pond

Ducks squat at the edge of clouds.
Kites glide stealthily like pikes.
A white yacht makes a voyage
To nowhere. Two small boys
Poke sticks into their jelly likenesses.
Parents, dogs, foreigners, predatory
Girls stand round the pond
Like minutes on a clock.

Vicki Feaver

Broken Roots

Moving through the garden, brooding, trowel held like
a weapon, I find a frail plant struggling in
a bleak and sunless corner. Kneeling to prise
it up the clod comes away and lies cold in
my pale palm. Broken roots trail, tremble in air
they've never known, and in the garden's silence
I recall how I was shifted from town to town,
uprooted, made to feel strange in strange places.

The memory camera whirrs its old movies,
stuttering images glut and blur behind
my eyes. Men in battered hats fork hay, sirens
wail down a long street, a woman bleeds beneath
a tram, on a strand wind whips sand into young
faces, hens scutter in a kitchen's darkness.
But to this there is no geography, no map
to read. Forgotten landscapes fade to greyness.

I fish for faces, dredge up fixed smiles which gaze
from ageing snapshots. I track my blood line back
through the years but the trail dries up, there are no
more people. I find no reason for being in
this silent place, and kneeling here on the damp
earth I come to a dead end. I stare at my
clenched fist. The frail plant, its roots, are crushed.
The clod crumbles, soil dribbles through my fingers
like days, days.

Wes Magee

Days

They come to us
Empty but not clean –
Like unrinsed bottles

Sides clouded
With a film
Of yesterday.

We can't keep them.
Our task is to fill up
And return.

There are no wages.
The reward is said to be
The work itself.

And if we question this,
Get angry, scream
At their round clock faces

Or try to break the glass,
We only hurt ourselves.
The days remain intact.

They wake us up
With light and leave us
In the dark.

For night is not
Their weakness – but a tease
To make us dream of death.

There is no end to days.
Only a cloth laid
Over a birdcage.

Vicki Feaver

Yorkshiremen in Pub Gardens

As they sit there, happily drinking,
their strokes, cancers and so forth are not in their
    minds.
Indeed, what earthly good would thinking
about the future (which is Death) do? Each summer
    finds
beer in their hands in big pint glasses.
And so their leisure passes.

Perhaps the older ones allow some inkling
into their thoughts. Being hauled, as a kid, upstairs to
    bed
screaming for a teddy or a tinkling
musical box, against their will. Each Joe or Fred
wants longer with the life and lasses.
And so their time passes.

Second childhood; and 'Come in, number 80!'
shouts inexorably the man in charge of the boating
    pool.
When you're called you must go, matey,
so don't complain, keep it all calm and cool,
there's masses of time yet, masses, masses . . .
And so their life passes.

Gavin Ewart

Uncle Edward's Affliction

Uncle Edward was colour-blind;
We grew accustomed to the fact.
When he asked someone to hand him
The green book from the window-seat
And we observed its bright red cover
Either apathy or tact
Stifled comment. We passed it over.
Much later, I began to wonder
What a curious world he wandered in,
Down streets where pea-green pillar boxes
Grinned at a fire-engine as green;
How Uncle Edward's sky at dawn
And sunset flooded marshy green.
Did he ken John Peel with his coat so green
And Robin Hood in Lincoln red?
On country walks avoid being stung
By nettles hot as a witch's tongue?
What meals he savoured with his eyes:
Green strawberries and fresh red peas,
Green beef and greener burgundy.
All unscientific, so it seems:
His world was not at all like that,
So those who claim to know have said.
Yet, I believe, in war-smashed France
He must have crawled from neutral mud
To lie in pastures dark and red
And seen, appalled, on every blade
The rain of innocent green blood.

Vernon Scannell

Old Men

When there was a war they went to war,
when there was peace they went to the labour exchange,
or carried hods on an hour's notice.
If their complaints were heard in Heaven
no earthly sign was given.

They have suffered obscurely a bleak recurring dream
many lifetimes long. Wounded and gassed
for noble causes they were not thought fit to under-
    stand
made idle to satisfy the greed of their betters
lectured when it suited the State
ignored when it suited the State
flattered by comedians
studied by young sociologists,
they have survived to be cosseted by the Regional
    Hospital Board.

They sit on a low stone wall in front of The Home
in an afternoon sun that shines like new,
grateful to have been allowed so much.
They puff black pipes.
Their small eyes see dead wives and children who
    emigrated.
They talk about the evening meal
and that old bugger George who's going senile.

When they walk in they tread gingerly,
not trusting the earth to stay beneath them for much
    longer.

Tony Connor

Note for the Future

When I get old
don't dress me in
frayed jackets
and too-short trousers,
and send me out
to sit around bowling-greens
in summer.
Don't give me just enough
to exist on, and expect me
to like passing
the winter days
in the reading-room
of the local library, waiting
my turn to read
last night's local paper.
Shoot me!
Find a reason, any reason,
say I'm a troublemaker,
or can't take care of myself
and live in a dirty room.
If you're afraid
of justifying my execution
on those terms,
tell everyone I leer
at little girls, and then
shoot me!
I don't care why you do it,
but do it,
and don't leave me
to walk to corner-shops
counting my coppers,
or give me a pass to travel cheap
at certain times, like a leper.

Jim Burns

'a hard day's work'

a hard day's work
lends a man dignity

and he is never out of debt

Alan Jackson

The Kitchen
(For my grandmother)

Scrubbed like a cube of sunlight,
the kitchen walls and the kitchen floor
whitened throughout my childhood,
spreading like an October morning

wild with blackberries and streams.
At the sink, Grandmother laundered.
At the table, Grandmother read and sewed,
dissecting the new neighbours.

On the doorstep, she dreamed of trees.
And the kitchen whitened around her,
like a cube of scrubbed sunlight,
white wood and red tiles.

In the end, it was ripe with silence,
this room stilled to a glow,
smelling like an October morning,
wild with blackberries and streams.

William Bedford

One Flesh

Lying apart now, each in a separate bed,
He with a book, keeping the light on late,
She like a girl dreaming of childhood,
All men elsewhere – it is as if they wait
Some new event: the book he holds unread,
Her eyes fixed on the shadows overhead.

Tossed up like flotsam from a former passion,
How cool they lie. They hardly ever touch,
Or if they do it is like a confession
Of having little feeling – or too much.
Chastity faces them, a destination
For which their whole lives were a preparation.

Strangely apart, yet strangely close together,
Silence between them like a thread to hold
And not wind in. And time itself's a feather
Touching them gently. Do they know they're old,
These two who are my father and mother
Whose fire from which I came, has now grown cold?

Elizabeth Jennings

The Son

Lying awake, in the room
over their room, the voices
drifting up through the floor-boards –
a grinding, night-long quarrel
between the two who made you.
How can you bear to listen?

A shared bed, a shared hatred
to warm it in the small hours.
Four living children, one dead.
Five proofs of something, one you
who lie there above them. Grey
coals hiss as the fire burns low.

Edward Lucie-Smith

Flood

My father's temper was as hot
as Seville in August, black
as a bull's hide, harsh
as Jerez leather.

What little heat remains
runs in arteries
constricted as Lancashire canals.

My mother was moderate, calm,
white-skinned, fair.
She went dancing in the 1920s,
asked permission to cut her hair.

Now, she has to rely on tears,
and even they fall
too frequently
to count.

I think she weeps to keep my father flowing,
and he, knowing,
watches the flood
that will take them both
down.

Olga Benjamin

Death of a Film Star
(For John Owen)

the first time we both saw him die
he was an old man
tired by the campfire
talking of women and of home
caught by the arrow's kick
he coughed and fell in those days
no one bled
a few months later
in an alleyway and the rain
a gunman caught him
in the pistol's sudden slam
his last words snapped and tossed away

middle-aged we saw him strangled
then a youth poisoned in a french hotel
next the gestapo caught him in a country lane
he froze he drowned when pirates sank his ship
then re-appeared
a bandit in a false moustache

now in the papers they say he died
a pensioner in an old hotel.
not true of course
we wait for his true death
a young man smiling
as the indians attack

Richard Hill

When I Am Dead

I desire that my body be
properly clothed. In such things
as I may like at the time.

And in the pockets may there be
placed such things as I use at the time
as, pen, camera, wallet, file.

And I desire to be laid on my side
Face down: since I have bad dreams
If I lie on my back
No one shall see my face when I die.

And beside me shall lie
my stone pig
with holes in his eyes.

And the coffin shall be as big as a crate.
No thin box
for the bones only.

Let there be room for a rat to come in.

And see that my cat, if I have one then,
shall have my liver.
He will like that.

And lay in food for
a week and a day:
chocolate, meat, beans, cheese.

And let all lie in
the wind and the rain.
And on the eighth day burn.

And the ash
scatter as the wind decides.
And the stone and metal be dug in the ground.

This is my will.

George MacBeth

A Case of Murder

They should not have left him there alone,
Alone that is except for the cat.
He was only nine, not old enough
To be left alone in a basement flat,
Alone, that is, except for the cat.
A dog would have been a different thing,
A big gruff dog with slashing jaws,
But a cat with round eyes mad as gold,
Plump as a cushion with tucked-in paws –
Better have left him with a fair-sized rat!
But what they did was leave him with a cat.
He hated that cat; he watched it sit,
A buzzing machine of soft black stuff,
He sat and watched and he hated it,
Snug in its fur, hot blood in a muff,
And its mad gold stare and the way it sat
Crooning dark warmth: he loathed all that.
So he took Daddy's stick and he hit the cat.
Then quick as a sudden crack in glass
It hissed, black flash, to a hiding place
In the dust and dark beneath the couch,
And he followed the grin on his new-made face,
A wide-eyed, frightened snarl of a grin,
And he took the stick and he thrust it in,
Hard and quick in the furry dark,
The black fur squealed and he felt his skin
Prickle with sparks of dry delight.
Then the cat again came into sight,
Shot for the door that wasn't quite shut,

But the boy, quick too, slammed fast the door:
The cat, half-through, was cracked like a nut
And the soft black thud was dumped on the floor.
Then the boy was suddenly terrified
And he bit his knuckles and cried and cried;
But he had to do something with the dead thing there.
His eyes squeezed beads of salty prayer
But the wound of fear gaped wide and raw;
He dared not touch the thing with his hands
So he fetched a spade and shovelled it
And dumped the load of heavy fur
In the spidery cupboard under the stair
Where it's been for years, and though it died
It's grown in that cupboard and its hot low purr
Grows slowly louder year by year:
There'll not be a corner for the boy to hide
When the cupboard swells and all sides split
And the huge black cat pads out of it.

Vernon Scannell

WATCHWORDS

Watchwords

watch the words
watch words the
watchword is
watch words are
sly as boots
ifyoutakeyoureyesoffthemforaminute

up

and   they're   and

away

allover

the

place
Roger McGough

Assass in

there is an assass
in the house
hold me tight
hold me tight
hold me and my shad
oh love will surely
find a way out
side a policeman
disguised as an owl
snuggles down in the old oak
not giving a hoot
and dreams of policewomen
disguised as mice

Roger McGough

Nobody Knows
How She

the body floating in the
water   no signs of

foul   they found one
shoe a notebook

play the body of
a woman on the

11 o'clock news

wearing the same
nobody dress

floating floating

Lyn Lifshin

Shoes

shoes come from leather leather
comes from cows come from milk no
no milk comes from cows come
from shoes baby shoes
                    come
from there to here hear
the shoes of blind childrens shoes
shuffling tripping a blind child falls into a cement
    mixer
a deaf child is crushed by the ambulance racing to the
    blind child who is the child of some dumb man who
    makes shoes

that evening he cries over a piece of leather stained
    with milk
the tear marks make a pattern he tries to read to read
he wants to cut the leather into the shape of a ginger-
    bread man

he wants very much to have his child back
to ride on the cows back

Tom Raworth

35 feet deep in the wet language

35 feet deep in the wet language
my love lies buried, delectable;
my love lies blue without breathing
35 feet deep in the wet language.

O to be air
and around her!
But I'm not air and she's not mine.
And so I pour

yet more words into the hole,
lovingly, lovingly;
35 feet, 50 feet, 100 feet, 1000 feet
the words rise over her, all begging her to breathe.

But how can she breathe, thus all cemented up?
Forgive me my pleas without end, forgive me these 92
   more words, my love . . .

John O. Thompson

What?

Where
man has not been
to give
them names
objects
on desert islands
do not
know what they are.
Taking no chances
they stand still
and wait
quietly excited
for hundreds
of
thousands of
years.

Ivor Cutler

Alone

If
you are mortar
it is
hard
to feel well-disposed
towards
the
two bricks
you are squashed
between
or
even
a sense of
community.

Ivor Cutler

The Five to Six Results

hurt results away
north ground flames
at home
matchplay to torture
in nets old bridgford
showed a leg in coming
events
sanctuary nil

Spike Hawkins

Nest

The giant bird has left the attic
Alone the attic empty
Neat no longer a nest in the pillows
You're not there
The bird has flown
The bird has no longer a weekend
We are alone
The life is dry in the room
As a garden whose little girl swims
with the cat into the pool
Onto a plain of poplars full of all
the times you reached the cinema
and found the bird in the front
row in love with the ice cream
                    dragon

Spike Hawkins

The Road

The road to Hell gets the worm.
The road to Hell gathers no moss.
The road to Hell leaves no stone unturned.

The road to Hell from little acorns grows.
The road to Hell is paved with rolling stones.
The road to Hell waits for no man.

The road to Hell takes the hindmost.
The road to Hell has its day.
The road to Hell spoils the broth.

The road to Hell has a silver lining:
The road to Hell wasn't built in a day.
On the road to Hell, do as the Romans do.

Henry Mathews

Sea's cape

I
see
gulls
Icy
gulls
I see
gulls screaming
– Aye –
I see seagulls
screaming, see
Ai YUY –
scream

. . . 'Ice *CREAM*'
the seagulls
seem to scream
Hi Hi *eee*
Ye – Icy seagulls!

I see

Gulls   see

eyes

cream

Michael Horovitz

In Memoriam, Winter 1979

Winter is icummen in,
Lhude sing Goddamm
Ezra Pound

In Leyton the blizzards
Are hazards for buzzards,
And in Leighton Buzzard
They bother the lizards.

In Luton the bollards
Snowed under and scissored
Buzz at the poor buggers
Not splat to the gizzard

By weather conditions
Which have blitzed soccer's wizards,
And taken their toll
Of bowling greens too

– Though I do not think
This last fact
Has been commemorated
In a poem

Until now.

Michael Horovitz

Sir Henry Morgan's Song

we came to the boat and blew the horn
we blew the boom and came to the island
we came the innocent and cut the cackle
we cut the tackle and stripped the bosun
we stripped the brandy and shaved the parrot
we shaved the part and shut the trap
we shut the shroud and bent the log
we bent the ocean and swung the lead
we sung the lumber and blued the lamp
we blued the thunder and crawled the crazes
we crawled Mither Carey and came to St Elmo
we came to the Horn and blew the boat

Edwin Morgan

Blue Toboggans

scarves for the apaches
wet gloves for snowballs
whoops for white clouds
and blue toboggans

stamping for a tingle
lamps for four o'clock
steamed glass for buses
and blue toboggans

tuning-forks for Wenceslas
white fogs for Prestwick
mince pies for the Eventides
and blue toboggans

TV for the lonely
a long haul for heaven
a shilling for the gas
and blue toboggans

Edwin Morgan

The First Men on Mercury

– We come in peace from the third planet.
Would you take us to your leader?

– Bawr stretter! Bawr. Bawr. Stretterhawl?

– This is a little plastic model
of the solar system, with working parts.
You are here and we are there and we
are now here with you, is this clear?

– Gawl horrop. Bawr. Abawrhannahanna!

– Where we come from is blue and white
with brown, you see we call the brown
here 'land', the blue is 'sea', and the white
is 'clouds' over land and sea, we live
on the surface of the brown land,
all around is sea and clouds. We are 'men'.
Men come –

– Glawp men! Gawrbenner menko. Menhawl?

– Men come in peace from the third planet
which we call 'earth'. We are earthmen.
Take us earthmen to your leader.

– Thmen? Thmen? Bawr. Bawrhossop.
Yuleeda tan hanna. Harrabost yuleeda.

– I am the yuleeda. You see my hands,
we carry no benner, we come in peace.
The spaceways are all stretterhawn.

– Glawn peacemen all horrabhanna tantko!
Tan come at'mstrossop. Glawp yuleeda!

– Atoms are peacegawl in our harraban
Menbat worrabost from tan hannahanna.

– You men we know bawrhossoptant. Bawr.
We know yuleeda. Go strawg backspetter quick.

– We cantantabawr, rantingko backspetter now!

– Banghapper now! Yes, third planet back.
Yuleeda will go back blue, white, brown
nowhanna! There is no more talk.

– Gawl han fasthapper?

– No. You must go back to your planet.
Go back in peace, take what you have gained
but quickly.

– Stretterworra gawl, gawl . . .

– Of course, but nothing is ever the same,
now is it? You'll remember Mercury.

Edwin Morgan

The New, Fast, Automatic Daffodils
(New variation on Wordsworth's 'Daffodils')

I wandered lonely as
THE NEW, FAST DAFFODIL
   FULLY AUTOMATIC
that floats on high o'er vales and hills
The Daffodil is generously dimensioned to accommo-
date four adult passengers
10,000 saw I at a glance
Nodding their new anatomically shaped heads in
sprightly dance
Beside the lake beneath the trees
     in three bright modern colours
red, blue and pigskin
The Daffodil de luxe is equipped with a host of useful
accessories
including windscreen wiper and washer with joint
control
A Daffodil doubles the enjoyment of touring at home
or abroad

in vacant or in pensive mood
SPECIFICATION:
   Overall width   1·44m (57″)
   Overall height   1·38m (54·3″)
   Max. speed   105 km/hr (65m.p.h.)
     (also cruising speed)

DAFFODIL
  RELIABLE — ECONOMICAL
DAFFODIL
  THE BLISS OF SOLITUDE
DAFFODIL
  The Variomatic Inward Eye
Travelling by Daffodil you can relax and enjoy every
  mile of the journey.

(Cut-up of Wordsworth's poem plus Dutch motor-car
leaflet)

Adrian Henri

The Computer's Ode to Autumn

Season of probabilities! Of seeds
Of sun and rain and soil and stony ground.
This is the season when I estimate
How many seeds will fall, how many live.
$2{\cdot}49 \times 10^7$ acorns
$3{\cdot}52 \times 10^5$ horse chestnuts
$1{\cdot}07 \times 10^8$ beech seeds.
These are last year's figures.
For all of Britain. We need expect no change.

There are as many oaks this year as last.
Surrey is full of beeches, Hampshire is full,
Yorkshire is losing alders, Leicestershire
Has fewer sycamores, Kent fewer birches.
Even the seeds that fall in humus, sprout
And turn to saplings will appear next spring,
Wave an imploring leaf, and die. Three seeds
Out of each million reach maturity.
There is no further room for trees in England

I am not callous, not indifferent.
Such minute probabilities must move me.
Each year I estimate, each year I grieve.
For Autumn makes me lyrical. Each year
I think about these numbers, and despair.
How many seeds will rot, how many shrivel,
How many oh how many will be eaten.
Season of such improbabilities,
Of such nostalgic numbers! Only I
Know how unlikely. I am the poet of autumn.

Laurence Lerner

New Body

As you saw my leopards coat
I was a tiger

As you felt my bears claw
I was a snake

As you stroked my cats fur
I was a fish

As you built me a lions cage
I was a worm

As you gripped mountains
I was a stream

As you crept tunnels
I was the sun

As you sought warmth
I was snow

As you expected thunder
I was calm

As you expected blood
I was stone

As you expected shape
I was air

As you looked
I was invisible

As you felt
I was near

When I appear
you tremble

Tom Pickard

MANIC depressant

SOMETIMES I'M HAPPY
sometimes i'm sad;
SoMeTiMeS i'M HsAaPdPY.

Kim Dammers

The Way You Dance Is the Way I Live

dancehall   the
              people   all   doing

the
              same   each
                            things

  one   pivoting   the

same   graceless
                            arc
                                  of
                                  aching empty
                                              hope
                                                    less
                                                          hope

  strange   but   they   never   meet
        the   way   they   dance
    is   the   way   i
                        live

Martin Ward

BEING IN LOVE

Being-in-love

you are so very beautiful
i cannot help admiring
your eyes so often sadnessful
and lips so kissinspiring

i think about my being-in-love
and touch the flesh you wear so well
i think about my being-in-love
and wish you were as well
                              as well
and wish you were as well

Roger McGough

Love is ...

Love is feeling cold in the back of vans
Love is a fanclub with only two fans
Love is walking holding paintstained hands
Love is

Love is fish and chips on winter nights
Love is blankets full of strange delights
Love is when you don't put out the light
Love is

Love is the presents in Christmas shops
Love is when you're feeling Top of the Pops
Love is what happens when the music stops
Love is

Love is white panties lying all forlorn
Love is a pink nightdress still slightly warm
Love is when you have to leave at dawn
Love is

Love is you and love is me
Love is a prison and love is free
Love's what's there when you're away from me
Love is ...

Adrian Henri

*Song for a Beautiful Girl
Petrol-Pump Attendant
on the Motorway*

I wanted your soft verges
But you gave me the hard shoulder.

Adrian Henri

Poem

Get your tongue
out
of my mouth;
I'm kissing you
goodbye.

Ted Kooser

The Vanished Fiancée

Went out drinking with
  her two bridesmaids
Friday night and
  hasn't been seen
since by her to-be-
  groom or her mother.
Wedding'd been set for
  Saturday noon.
Police understand she's
  with a boyfriend
somewhere in Birmingham.
  She's sixteen.

'We have had e-
  nough and we don't want
any more' is
  all the jilted boy's
father will say to
  newsmen. But her
brother still hopes
  the wedding'll take place.
Meanwhile Birmingham
  concrete dances in
maid-wide, stray-bright
  runaway eyes.

John O. Thompson

3 Acts

I watch you watching her.
She laughs at you.
I pull a face.
They watch us.
Bated breath.

You look at me to
make sure you're still here.
She cannot look
for fear of looking back.
They clap.

She glares at me.
You stare at me
to see what face I make.
Give in to both. Both take.
Three acts.

I look through you for doors.
She bolts her eyes.
You look through her at
me burning curtains.
They fidget at the plot.

I put a blindfold on.
You tear it off. She
shines a light too bright
in them.
The audience go wild.

Carol Ann Duffy

Our Love Now

I said,
    observe how the wound heals in time,
    how the skin slowly knits
    and once more becomes whole.
    The cut will mend, and such
    is our relationship.

I said,
    observe the scab of the scald,
    the red burnt flesh is ugly,
    but it can be hidden.
    In time it will disappear,
    Such is our love, such is our love.

I said,
    remember how when you cut your hair,
    you feel different, and somehow incomplete.
    But the hair grows – before long
    it is always the same.
    Our beauty together is such.

I said,
    listen to how the raging storm
    damages the trees outside.
    The storm is frightening
    but it will soon be gone.
    People will forget it ever existed.
    The breach in us can be mended.

She said,
    Although the wound heals
    and appears cured, it is not the same.
    There is always a scar,
    a permanent reminder.
    Such is our love now.

She said,
    Although the burn will no longer sting
    and we'll almost forget that it's there
    the skin remains bleached
    and a numbness prevails.
    Such is our love now.

She said,
    After you've cut your hair,
    it grows again slowly. During that time
    changes must occur,
    the style will be different.
    Such is our love now.

She said,
    Although the storm is temporary
    and soon passes,
    it leaves damage in its wake
    which can never be repaired.
    The tree is forever dead.
    Such is our love.

Martyn Lowery

The Influence

I wish that woman in the
garden would stand still.

The trees, sky, fence,
rooftops across the field,

are perfect for painting,
piled up on top of each

other, in slabs of colour,
and all without movement,

but she insists on bobbing
up and down by the window.

Later, she'll be inside,
breaking up the tidiness

of the house, pushing the
clock back an inch, sliding

a chair forward, and leaving
papers scattered all around.

This poem, too, has been
disturbed. It could have

become a cool description
of the garden, but instead

it has turned out to be
yet another portrait of her.

Jim Burns

Cabbages

the young girls are cutting the cabbages
green leaves closed over white hearts

they are cutting with knives that gleam
like moonlight, like rings, like tears

the young girls are stripping the cabbage beds
their flesh is the warm brown of fertile earth

What will open their green leaves
or pierce their white hearts?

knives or moonlight
rings or tears.

Dave Calder

Launderette

And they of course not knowing
that dreams were being rinsed out beside them
sat waiting for red lights and signs
and cups of soap powder.
While the sheets I had held you in
had you washed out
silently, while more lights flashed.
I began to know the rhythms
of the clothes as embryolike, they
wound into each other, became
a hot snowball of cloth, slithering
round behind glass, round
like falling angels or
dancing couples.
Second cupfuls brought the sea
waves dashing high against
the window, spray reaching the
glass beach.
And for us, no sea.
Bubbles continued
into a white wall hiding
the clothes from me.
Blankness all washed out
and hidden.
The small you inside the window
was disappearing.
It's too late to drag them out and ask for my
money and dirt back, for wanting the hot white
sheets and our electric moments.
Tenderly I dried them in the cabinet
and took them home,
warm like new bread,

leaving the others to watch their dreams
slowly murdered into whiteness
for new surgical beds.

Pat Jourdan

After the Fall

Adam.
    Lady
    I've not had a moment's love
    Since I was expelled.

    Let me in.

Eve.
    Lord
    I've not had a moment's rest
    Since I was a rib.

    Put me back.

Anne Stevenson

Sociosexual Primer for Children (of all ages)

BIRTH
No one ever completely recovers from it.
It helps considerably if one is born
the right way up, but
as I have forgotten the difference
between right and wrong, up and down,
you will have to ask someone else
for directions.

MOTHER
Baby ducks can become attached
to a bright red ball. Your
bright red ball may have hard hands
that sting. Try not to become attached
to hands that sting, as in
later life soft and gentle hands
may not fulfil you.

FATHER
Has complete control of no.
Always remember that one day you
will be able to deny others
simple pleasures. The pain
you may inflict on those who love you
will increase the bigger you become.

PUBERTY

You will discover your own body, and
if you are lucky others will also discover
your body. Far too much importance
is attached to sex, but
if you are lucky you may never
find this out.

INTERCOURSE

Takes place between man and woman
(most of the time). Few people
ever give the slightest sign
that it is only intended for reproduction;
in fact most become very surprised
when reproduction shows the slightest sign.

LOVE

Increases in direct proportion
to the lack of interest of the beloved.
For complete information listen
to popular music; every facet
is thoroughly worked to death.

MARRIAGE

Henry Graham

Somewhere between Heaven and Woolworth's
A Song

She keeps kingfishers in their cages
And goldfish in their bowls,
She is lovely and is afraid
Of such things as growing cold.

She's had enough men to please her
Though they were more cruel than kind
And their love an act in isolation,
A form of pantomime.

She says she has forgotten
The feelings that she shared
At various all-night parties
Among the couples on the stairs,

For among the songs and dancing
She was once open wide,
A girl dressed in denim
With boys dressed in lies.

She's eating roses on toast with tulip butter,
Praying for her mirror to stay young;
On its no longer gilted surface
This message she has scrawled:

'O somewhere between Heaven and Woolworth's
I live I love I scold,
I keep kingfishers in their cages
And goldfish in their bowls.'

Brian Patten

A Blade of Grass

You ask for a poem.
I offer you a blade of grass.
You say it is not good enough.
You ask for a poem.

I say this blade of grass will do.
It has dressed itself in frost,
It is more immediate
Than any image of my making.

You say it is not a poem,
It is a blade of grass and grass
Is not quite good enough.
I offer you a blade of grass.

You are indignant.
You say it is too easy to offer grass.
It is absurd.
Anyone can offer a blade of grass.

You ask for a poem.
And so I wrote you a tragedy about
How a blade of grass
Becomes more and more difficult to offer,

And about how as you grow older
A blade of grass
Becomes more difficult to accept.

Brian Patten

Sometimes It Happens

And sometimes it happens that you are friends and
  then
You are not friends,
And friendship has passed.
And whole days are lost and among them
A fountain empties itself.

And sometimes it happens that you are loved and then
You are not loved,
And love is past.
And whole days are lost and among them
A fountain empties itself into the grass.

And sometimes you want to speak to her and then
You do not want to speak,
Then the opportunity has passed.
Your dreams flare up, they suddenly vanish.

And also it happens that there is nowhere to go and
  then
There is somewhere to go,
Then you have bypassed.
And the years flare up and are gone,
Quicker than a minute.

So you have nothing.
You wonder if these things matter and then
They cease to matter,
And caring is past.
And a fountain empties itself into the grass.

Brian Patten

Absence

I visited the place where we last met.
Nothing was changed, the gardens were well-tended
The fountains sprayed their usual steady jet;
There was no sign that anything had ended
And nothing to instruct me to forget.

The thoughtless birds that shook out of the trees,
Singing an ecstasy I could not share,
Played cunning in my thoughts. Surely in these
Pleasures there could not be a pain to bear
Or any discord shake the level breeze.

It was because the place was just the same
That made your absence seem a savage force,
For under all the gentleness there came
An earthquake tremor: fountain, birds and grass
Were shaken by my thinking of your name.

Elizabeth Jennings

My Version

I hear that since you left me
Things go from bad to worse,
That the Good Lord, quite rightly,
Has set a signal curse

On you, your house and lover.
(I learn, moreover, he
Proves twice as screwed-up, selfish
And sodden, dear, as me.)

They say your days are tasteless,
Flattened, disjointed, thinned.
Across the waste my absence,
Love's skeleton, has grinned.

Perfect. I trust my sources
Of information are sound?
Or is it just some worthless rumour
I've been spreading round?

Kit Wright

Every Day in Every Way
(Dr Coué: Every day in every way
I grow better and better)

When I got up this morning
I thought the whole thing through:
Thought, Who's the hero, the man of the day?
Christopher, it's you.

With my left arm I raised my right arm
High above my head:
Said, Christopher, you're the greatest.
Then I went back to bed.

I wrapped my arms around me,
No use counting sheep.
I counted legions of myself
Walking on the deep.

The sun blazed on the miracle,
The blue ocean smiled:
We like the way you operate,
Frankly, we like your style.

Dreamed I was in a meadow,
Angels singing hymns,
Fighting the nymphs and shepherds
Off my holy limbs.

A girl leaned out with an apple,
Said, You can taste it for free.
I never touch the stuff, dear,
I'm keeping myself for me.

Dreamed I was in heaven,
God said, Over to you,
Christopher, you're the greatest!
And O, it's true, it's true!

I like my face in the mirror,
I like my voice when I sing.
My girl says it's just infatuation –
I know it's the real thing.

Kit Wright

A CAT,
A HORSE AND THE SUN

A Cat, a Horse and the Sun

a cat mistrusts the sun
keeps out of its way
only where sun and shadows meet
it moves

a horse loves the sun
it basks all day
snorts
and beats its hooves

the sun likes horses
but hates cats
that is why it makes hay
and heats tin rooves

Roger McGough

The Trees

The trees are coming into leaf
Like something almost being said;
The recent buds relax and spread,
Their greenness is a kind of grief.

Is it that they are born again
And we grow old? No, they die too.
Their yearly trick of looking new
Is written down in rings of grain.

Yet still the unresting castles thresh
In fullgrown thickness every May.
Last year is dead, they seem to say,
Begin afresh, afresh, afresh.

Philip Larkin

Frost on the Shortest Day

A heavy frost last night,
The longest night of the year,
Makes the land at first light
Look spruced up for death,
Incurably white.

But the earth moving fast
Tips the shadow across
The field. It rolls past
Sheep who hold their ground
And into the hedge at last.

Not far behind, a track
Of frost is following
That the sun cannot lick
Completely green in time,
Before night rolls back.

Patricia Beer

Full Moon and Little Frieda

A cool small evening shrunk to a dog bark and the
  clank of a bucket –

And you listening.
A spider's web, tense for the dew's touch.
A pail lifted, still and brimming – mirror
To tempt a first star to tremor.

Cows are going home in the lane there, looping the
  hedges with their warm wreaths of breath –
A dark river of blood, many boulders,
Balancing unspilled milk.

'Moon!' you cry suddenly, 'Moon! Moon!'

The moon has stepped back like an artist gazing
  amazed at a work
That points at him amazed.

Ted Hughes

The Harvest Moon

The flame-red moon, the harvest moon,
Rolls along the hills, gently bouncing,
A vast balloon,
Till it takes off, and sinks upward
To lie in the bottom of the sky, like a gold doubloon.

The harvest moon has come,
Booming softly through heaven, like a bassoon.
And earth replies all night, like a deep drum.

So people can't sleep,
So they go out where elms and oak trees keep
A kneeling vigil, in a religious hush.
The harvest moon has come!

And all the moonlit cows and all the sheep
Stare up, petrified, while the moon swells
Filling heaven, as if red hot, and sailing
Closer and closer like the end of the world.

Till the gold fields of stiff wheat
Cry 'We are ripe, reap us!' and the rivers
Sweat from the melting hills.

Ted Hughes

Cultivators

We,
who work with earth and steel
and feel winter frozen in our hands
where fields are looms,
weave the patterns of crops;
damp loam flows like silk
through shuttling metal.

And our hills,
with their wild uncurbable wills
may be hard to till
but are easy to love,
steep work weakens the tractor
but strengthens the heart.

Susan Taylor

To Winter

Cattle are a gentle tribe asking no favour
but a bale of hay to share
on a well tossed bed of straw
when clay turns cold
        and bitter wind whines
          dancing over flesh with metalled heels.

I had their serenity, once
wading through the tranquil munching
plastered with their filth,
but now I fold myself against the frost
for it bites deeper.
Leaves and flowers raised in soft earth
cringe, dying in its hardness
        and white grasses dry as bone
         all point in one direction.

Susan Taylor

Revelation

I remember once being shown the black bull
when a child at the farm for eggs and milk.
They called him Bob – as though perhaps
you could reduce a monster
with the charm of a friendly name.
At the threshold of his outhouse, someone
held my hand and let me peer inside.
At first, only black
and the hot reek of him. Then he was immense,
his edges merging with the darkness, just
a big bulk and a roar to be really scared of,
a trampling, and a clanking tense with the chain's jerk.
His eyes swivelled in the great wedge of his tossed head.
He roared his rage. His nostrils gaped like wounds.

And in the yard outside,
oblivious hens picked their way about.
The faint and rather festive tinkling
behind the mellow stone and hasp was all they knew
of that Black Mass, straining at his chains.
I had always half-known he existed –
this antidote and Anti-Christ his anarchy
threatened the eggs, well rounded, self-contained –
and the placidity of milk.

I ran, my pigtails thumping on my back in fear,
past the big boys in the farm lane
who pulled the wings from butterflies and
blew up frogs with straws.
Past thorned hedge and harried nest,
scared of the eggs shattering –
only my small and shaking hand on the jug's rim
in case the milk should spill.

Liz Lochhead

First Calf

It's a long time since I saw
The afterbirth strung on the hedge
As if the wind smarted
And streamed bloodshot tears.

Somewhere about
The cow stands with her head
Almost outweighing her tense sloped neck,
The calf hard at her udder.

The shallow bowls of her eyes
Tilt membrane and fluid.
The warm plinth of her snout gathers
A growth round moist nostrils.

Her hide stays warm in the wind,
Her wide eyes read nothing:
Those gay semaphores of hurt
Swaddle and flap on a bush.

Seamus Heaney

Praise of a Collie

She was a small dog, neat and fluid –
Even her conversation was tiny:
She greeted you with *bow*, never *bow-wow*.

Her sons stood monumentally over her
But did what she told them. Each grew grizzled
Till it seemed he was his own mother's grandfather.

Once, gathering sheep on a showery day,
I remarked how dry she was. Pollochan said, 'Ah,
It would take a very accurate drop to hit Lassie.'

And her tact – and tactics! When the sheep bolted
In an unforeseen direction, over the skyline
Came – who but Lassie, and not even panting.

She sailed in the dinghy like a proper sea-dog.
Where's a burn? – she's first on the other side.
She flowed through fences like a piece of black wind.

But suddenly she was old and sick and crippled . . .
I grieved for Pollochan when he took her a stroll
And put his gun to the back of her head.

Norman MacCaig

Time for the Knife

'You've a good one there,' Enright said.
Morrissey asked, 'Is he right for cutting yet?'
Enright lifted the terrier pup in his fist,
Slid the skin back on the gums
And fingered the neat fangs.

Caressing the brown and white head,
He handled the terrier's tail.

'Time for the knife,' he said.

The penknife from his waistcoat pocket
Flicked open. Twenty years of cutting tobacco
Had merely dented the blade.

'Let you hold the head.'
Morrissey gripped the skin behind the ears.

After he'd sharpened the knife on a stone
Enright stretched the tail
And started to cut.

It was over soon. Enright looked
At the severed tail in his fist
And pitched it into the grass.

The terrier pup
Howled as it fled,
Pursued by drops of its own blood
Regular as a pulse of pain.

For a while
It whimpered and cried alone
Like a woman mourning.

When the bleeding stopped
The stubby tail stuck up
Like a blunt warning.

Brendan Kennelly

Wasp Poem

Today I drowned a wasp that I
Found floating in my wine.
Its life no longer is its own,
but neither is it mine.
With cool precision turned by hate
I drowned it in the sink –
it struggled in the water
but I didn't stop to think.
I didn't feel a pang at all,
I didn't change my mind,
I didn't even, really, feel
that this was cruel, unkind.
If metamorphosis exists
perhaps a wasp I'll be
and I won't feel resentment
if you do the same to me.
I may regret the sunshine,
the pollen and the jam,
but I'll understand you're drowning me
because I'm what I am.

Verity Bargate

I Saw a Jolly Hunter

I saw a jolly hunter
   With a jolly gun
Walking in the country
   In the jolly sun.

In the jolly meadow
   Sat a jolly hare.
Saw the jolly hunter.
   Took jolly care.

Hunter jolly eager –
   Sight of jolly prey.
Forgot gun pointing
   Wrong jolly way.

Jolly hunter jolly head
   Over heels gone.
Jolly old safety catch
   Not jolly on.

Bang went the jolly gun
   Hunter jolly dead.
Jolly hare got clean away
   Jolly good, I said.

Charles Causley

A Lamb

Yes, I saw a lamb where they've built a new housing estate, where cars are parked in garages, where streets have names like Fern Hill Crescent

I saw a lamb where television aerials sprout from chimneypots, where young men gun their motor-bikes, where mothers watch from windows between lace curtains

I saw a lamb, I tell you, where lawns in front are neatly clipped, where cabbages and cauliflowers grow in back gardens, where doors and gates are newly painted

I saw a lamb, there in the dusk, the evening fires just lit, a scent of coal-smoke on the air, the sky faintly bruised by the sunset

yes, I saw it, I was troubled. I wanted to ask someone anyone, something, anything . . .

a man in a raincoat coming home from work but he was in a hurry. I went in at the next gate and rang the doorbell, and rang, but no one answered.

I noticed that the lights in the house were out. Some-one shouted at me from an upstairs window next door, 'They're on holiday. What do you want?' And I turned away because I wanted nothing

but a lamb in a green field.

Gael Turnbull

After We've Gone

Who will live in our house
After we've gone
Will they have green plastic
Instead of a lawn?

Who will live in our house
After the wars?
Will there be mutations
That crawl on all fours?

Will the shiny robot workers
Be dreaming strange, new dreams?
Will the pigeons, big as turkeys
Roost on our ancient beams?

Who will use our kitchen?
What will they cook?
Who will sleep in our room
And how will they look?

Will they feel our ghosts disturbing
Their cybernetic years
With the echoes of our laughter
And the shadows of our tears?

Will there still be lovers?
Who will sing our songs?
Who will live in our house
After we've gone?

Fran Landesman

SMITHEREENS

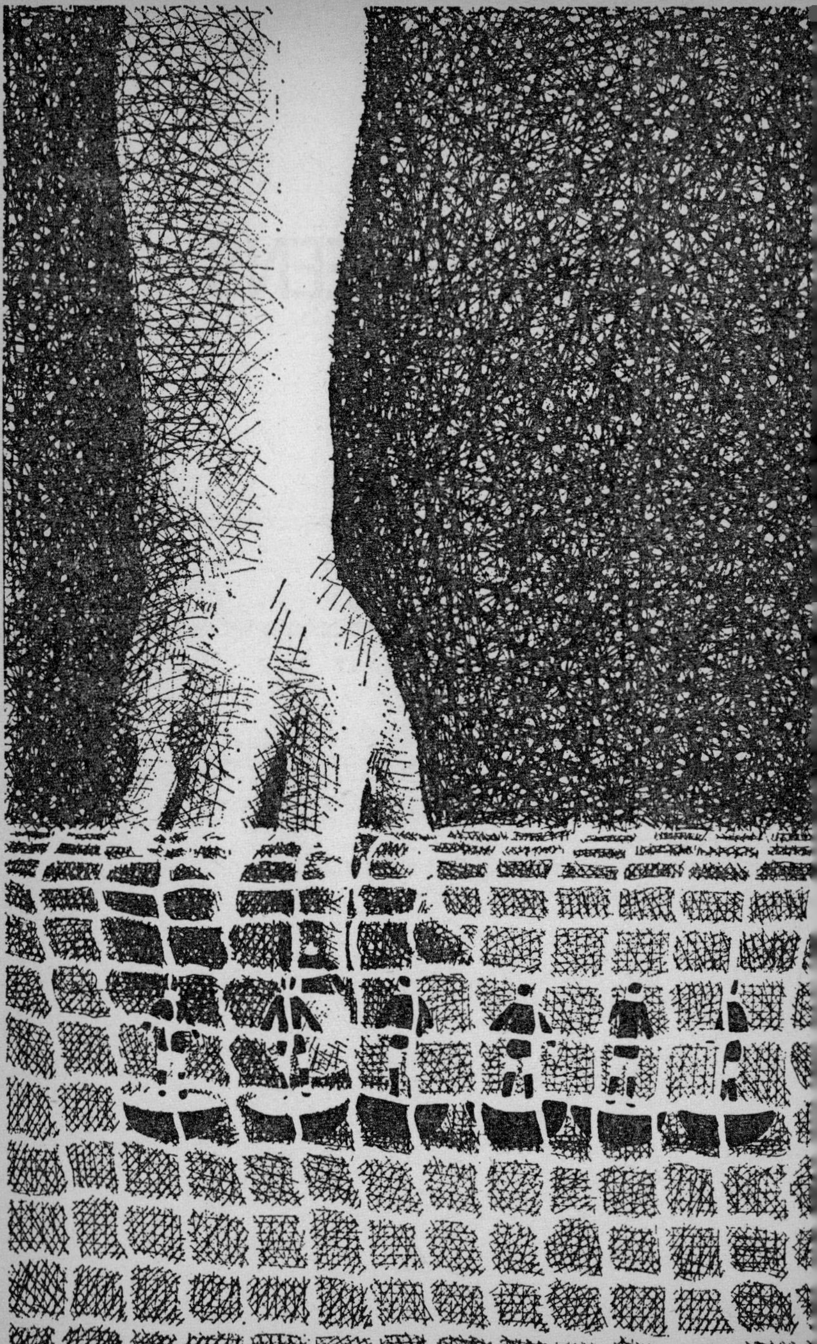

Smithereens

I spend my days
collecting smithereens.
I find them on buses
in department stores
and on busy pavements.

At restaurant tables
I pick up the leftovers
of polite conversation.
At railway stations
the tearful debris
of parting lovers.

I pocket my eavesdroppings
and store them away.
I make things out of them.
Nice things, sometimes.
Sometimes odd, like this.

Roger McGough

Scouts

Pontiac! Little Crow!
Joseph! Red Cloud!
Black Kettle!
Geronimo! Cochise! Crazy Horse!
Tecumseh! Powhatan!
Atahualpa!
Quetzalcoatl!

you're right
– this isn't Walsall, Staffs

Martin Hall

Tombstone Library

In Tombstone there was, it seems,
a public library
between the marshall's office
and the Silver Lode Saloon
On endless, silent afternoons
the clicking of the faro wheel
the tired piano's nervous tinkle
scratching the library's wooden walls
I like to think of them
the whores and gamblers
the faro dealers and the mining men
cool in the library's silent shade
whispering their way through 'Romance'
and 'Ancient History'
soft spurs jingling past the rows of books
the half-breed coughing gently over 'War and Peace'
And at the issue desk
a stocky figure in a bowler hat
'I'm sorry Mr Earp, this book is overdue'
He bends and fumbles
flicks out a coin, smiles
(his teeth are not yet film-star white)
dark and nervous as a cat
he turns and moves towards 'Mythology'

Richard Hill

Cowboy

I remember, on a long
Hot, summer, thirsty afternoon
Hiding behind a rock
With Wyatt Earp
(His glasses fastened on with sellotape)

The Sioux were massing for their last attack

We knew

No 7th Cavalry for us
No bugles blaring in the afternoon
I held my lone star pistol in my hand
Thinking
I was just seven and too young to die
Thinking

Save the last cap
For yourself.

Richard Hill

The Cowboy Poems

1

a hush falls
over the gambling tables

'this town ain't
big enough
for both of us'

during the night
six houses
and a saloon
mysteriously appear

2

'it's quiet'

'yeah
too quiet'

the projectionist pitches forward
clutching his chest

unmolested
the wagon train breaks camp
rolls on and on
and on and on
and on and on
and on and on

Alasdair Paterson

Cowboy Song

I come from Salem County
   Where the silver melons grow,
Where the wheat is sweet as an angel's feet
   And the zithering zephyrs blow.
I walk the blue bone-orchard
   In the apple-blossom snow,
When the teasy bees take their honeyed ease
   And the marmalade moon hangs low.

My Maw sleeps prone on the prairie
   In a boulder eiderdown,
Where the pickled stars in their little jam-jars
   Hang in a hoop to town.
I haven't seen Paw since a Sunday
   In eighteen seventy-three
When he packed his snap in a bitty mess-trap
   And said he'd be home by tea.

Fled is my fancy sister
   All weeping like the willow,
And dead is the brother I loved like no other
   Who once did share my pillow.
I fly the florid water
   Where run the seven geese round,
O the townsfolk talk to see me walk
   Six inches off the ground.

Across the map of midnight
   I trawl the turning sky,
In my green glass the salt fleets pass
   The moon her fire-float by.

The girls go gay in the valley
   When the boys come down from the farm,
Don't run, my joy, from a poor cowboy,
   I won't do you no harm.

The bread of my twentieth birthday
   I buttered with the sun,
Though I sharpen my eyes with lovers' lies
   I'll never see twenty-one.
Light is my shirt with lilies,
   And lined with lead my hood,
On my face as I pass is a plate of brass,
   And my suit is made of wood.

Charles Causley

I'll Stand the Lot of You

I'll stand the lot of you, I said
to the other kids. They said: Right!

I was Wolves 1957–58:
Finlayson; Stuart, Harris; Slater, Wright, Flowers;
Deeley, Broadbent, Murray, Mason, Mullen.
The other kids were Rest of the World:
Banks; Pele, Best; Best, Pele, Pele;
Best, Pele, Charlton, Pele, Best.
Jimmy Murray kicked off for Wolves.

Wolves were well on top in the opening minutes,
then Rest of the World broke away and scored
seven lucky goals. Wolves were in trouble!
But then tragedy struck Rest of the World:
Pele had to go and do their homework!
They were soon followed by Best and Charlton.
It was Wolves versus Banks!
Now Wolves played like a man possessed.
Soon they were on level terms!
Seven-all, and only minutes to go,
when suddenly – sensation! Banks went off
to watch the Cup Final on television!
Seconds later, a pinpoint Mullen centre
found Peter Broadbent completely unmarked
in front of goal. What a chance!

He missed it,
and Wolves trooped sadly off towards their bike.

Martin Hall

154

Incident at 'The Oval'

Here, sunk in memories of summer afternoons,
the few spectators are scattered singly around

the ground, and cricketers are patient gestures
half-lost in dazzle of sun. I rouse when the

ball smacks the boundary fence and go to retrieve it.
How its weight fits and grips my hand! I see the

frayed skin, shine gone, the seam bruised by flogging
    hooks
and cuts. In an hour it will be discarded.

I lob it back and the game strolls gently on.
The ball's red imprint slowly fades from my palm.

Over pints in pubs this tale would create yawns,
for it is a moment without meaning, a

private consolation to be recalled in the
howl of towns or when days fade to a sad close.

Wes Magee

D. H. Larwood

D. H. Larwood was the son of a Nottinghamshire
    miner.
He turned out to be the greatest novelist
and the greatest fast bowler
of his generation.

He let loose some astonishing books –
so fiery, passionate and outrageous
that he was banned down under.

His leg theory, his bodyline bowling,
had the critics gasping, all of the fast ones
that whistled round the head and heart.

You could say he intimidated the opposition.
He wasn't big – but full of life.

And now he's a classic, in the black and white photos.

Gavin Ewart

Sergeant Brown's Parrot

Many policemen wear upon their shoulders
cunning little radios. To pass away the time
They talk about the traffic to them, listen to the news,
And it helps them to Keep Down Crime

But Sergeant Brown, he wears upon his shoulder
A tall green parrot as he's walking up and down
And all the parrot says is 'Who's a-pretty-boy-then?'
'I am,' says Sergeant Brown.

Kit Wright

Unemployable

'I usth thu workth in the thircusth,'
He said,
Between the intermittent showers that emerged from
    his mouth.
'Oh,' I said, 'what did you do?'
'I usth thu catcth bulleth in my theeth.'

Gareth Owen

Did Anything Happen
at the Field Today, Dear?

The photograph shows
the frozen horror of that moment in time
the airship
booming into flame
the people
tiny
running to and fro arms
raised in fright
and looking closer we can see
one person
unconcerned
walking from the field
not having noticed the panic
behind him
striding
hands in pockets
head bowed in thought
he walks away
admiring the splendid polish
of his boots.

Richard Hill

Where have you been?

Where have you been?
I've been to the dance.

Where did you stay?
I stayed with a man.
You'll have to get married.
He's married already.

Your daughter is right.
The sergeant is married.

She's got to be punished.

She's washing her hair.

Your mother and I
have decided to drive
you and your dog to the desert.
When we find the right place
you'll shoot your dog.
Now go to bed.

I've set the clock.
We must teach her a lesson.

Christopher Logue

Spy Story

He awoke in a strange bed
In a strange room.
Beyond the grimed window
The street with no name
Was not one he knew
Though he had seen the same
Gaunt features in other places.
The slow and shuffling gait
Of the muffled passers-by,
The faces grey and strained,
The mongrel that sniffed and sidled.
Cocked a leg against a crate:
A stale, anonymous view.
Some of the shops were padlocked.
The windows barred.
He must not linger here
Breathing the alien air,
Smelling old scent and exile.
Stale tobacco and fear.
He descended to the street.
Head down and collar raised
And began to walk towards
The spot where he would meet
His enemy or accomplice,
Assassin or assistant.
Reprieve or last defeat.
He reached the public gardens
And sat on a bench to wait.
The minutes prowled past like prisoners.
It seemed he had come too late
Or mistaken the rendezvous;
Whatever the error, he knew

His contact was not going to show.
The day began to look older;
There was nowhere else to go.
The bickering wind grew colder
And from the darkening sky,
To rest lightly on head and shoulder,
Came the frail irresolute snow.

Vernon Scannell

Few

Alone tired halfdrunk hopeful
I staggered into the bogs
at Green Park station
and found 30 written on the wall

Appalled I lurched out
into the windy blaring Piccadilly night
thinking surely,
Surely there must be more of us than that . . .

Pete Brown

Robinson Crusoe

Before I left the island
     this book was in my head –
people must see you
     or you must tell people.
Man Friday hardly understood
     a word I said.
He walked in uninvited
     and sat down at my table.

He seemed to admire me greatly,
     my gun, my civilised ways,
then suddenly got bored.
     He might have slit my throat.
Nothing was settled between us.
     He would disappear for days,
then burst in, grinning,
     hanging on to my coat.

I will call it love in my book.
     The nearest word I can find.
When the vessel came to my rescue
     Man Friday had gone out
I don't know why I wanted
     so much to leave him behind.
I crouched in a cabin waiting
     to hear his awful shout.

imagined him bursting through
          the trees, his gesticulations
from the receding shore,
          ignored by captain and crew.
Nothing. Escape. The intercourse
          of polite nations.
How sweet to know what one is,
          what one is trying to do.

Last night a bad dream took me:
          Man Friday had pursued
so fast he was in England
          waiting on the quay.
No one could stop his grinning
          impulse to intrude
into private things, upsetting
          all that is sacred to me.

                    James Simmons

I like that stuff

Lovers lie around in it.
Broken glass is found in it
Grass
I like that stuff

Tuna fish get wrapped in it
Legs come wrapped in it
Nylon
I like that stuff

Eskimos and tramps chew it
Madame Tussaud gave status to it
Wax
I like that stuff

Elephants get sprayed with it
Scotch is made with it
Water
I like that stuff

Clergy are dumbfounded by it
Bones are surrounded by it
Flesh
I like that stuff

Harps are strung with it
Mattresses are sprung with it
Wire
I like that stuff

Cigarettes are lit by it
Pensioners get happy when they sit by it
Fire
I like that stuff

Dankworth's alto is made of it, most of it,
Scoobdedoo is composed of it
Plastic
I like that stuff

Man made fibres and raw materials
Old rolled gold and breakfast cereals
Platinum linoleum
I like that stuff

Skin on my hands
Hair on my head
Toenails on my feet
And linen on my bed

Well I like that stuff
Yes I like that stuff
   The earth
Is made of earth
   And I like that stuff

Adrian Mitchell

Cabbage

(After *I like that stuff* by Adrian Mitchell)

John Wayne died of it
People are terrified of it
cancer
I hate that stuff

Groucho was laid low with it
One in five of us will go with it
heart attack
I hate that stuff

Monroe's life turned sour on it
Hancock spent his last half hour on it
sleeping pills
I hate that stuff

Hendrix couldn't wait for it
Chemistshops stay open late for it
heroin
I hate that stuff

Mama Cass choked on it
Blankets get soaked in it
vomit
I hate that stuff

Women learn to live with it
No one can live without it
blood
I hate that stuff

Hospitals are packed with it
Saw my mother racked with it
          pain
     I hate that stuff

Few like to face the truth of it
We're the living proof of it
          death
     I hate that stuff

Schoolboys are forcefed with it
Cattle are served dead with it
          cabbage
     I hate that stuff

                    Roger McGough

Watch Your Step, I'm Drenched

In Manchester there are a thousand puddles.
Bus-queue puddles poised on slanting paving stones,
Railway puddles slouching outside stations,
Cinema puddles in ambush at the exits,
Zebra-crossing puddles in dips of the dark stripes –
They lurk in the murk
Of the north-western evening
For the sake of their notorious joke,
Their only joke – to soak
The tights or trousers of the citizens.
Each splash and consequent curse is echoed by
One thousand dark Mancunian puddle chuckles.

In Manchester there lives the King of Puddles,
Master of Miniature Muck Lakes,
The Shah of Slosh, Splendifero of Splash,
Prince, Pasha and Pope of Puddledom.
Where? Somewhere. The rain-headed ruler
Lies doggo, incognito,
Disguised as an average, accidental mini-pool.
He is scared as any other emperor,
For one night, all his soiled and soggy victims
Might storm his streets, assassination in their minds,
A thousand rolls of blotting paper in their hands,
And drink his shadowed, one-joke life away.

Adrian Mitchell

Poem for a Dead Poet

He was a poet he was.
A proper poet.
He said things
that made you think
and said them nicely.
He saw things
that you or I
could never see
and saw them clearly.
He had a way
with language.
Images flocked around
him like birds,
St Francis, he was,
of the words. Words?
Why he could almost make 'em talk.

Roger McGough

'Yes,' I said, 'but is it Art?'

Took me to the battlefield
saw the mushroom cloud
said 'We can see the colours even
when our heads are bowed.'
Showed me the destruction
the slaughter à la carte
said 'Isn't Nature wonderful.'
'Yes,' I said
'but is it Art?'

Took me to the scientist
opened up a phial
said 'This is only chicken-pox
and rhino bile.'
Showed me what it did to mice
said 'That's just a start
but isn't Nature wonderful.'
'Yes,' I said
'but is it Art?'

Took me to the hospital
pulled aside the sheet
said 'Look at that pulsating
listen to the beat.'
Showed me the incision
threw away the heart
said 'Isn't Nature wonderful.'
'Yes,' I said
'but is it Art?'

Took me to the tenement
opened every door
said 'Have you seen the copulation
practised by the poor?
We select the ones to breed
and we reject a part
but isn't Nature wonderful.'
'Yes,' I said
'but is it Art?'

Took me to the prison
threw away the key
said 'If you learn our lesson
you could still be free.'
Pointed out the spy holes
and my adaption chart
said 'Isn't Nature wonderful?'

'Yes,' I said.

Pete Morgan

What the Chairman Told Tom

POETRY? It's a hobby.
I run model trains.
Mr Shaw there breeds pigeons.

It's not work. You don't sweat.
Nobody pays for it.
You *could* advertise soap.

Art, that's opera; or repertory –
The Desert Song.
Nancy was in the chorus.

But to ask for twelve pounds a week –
married, aren't you? –
you've got a nerve.

How could I look a bus conductor
in the face
if I paid you twelve pounds?

Who says it's poetry, anyhow?
My ten year old
can do it *and* rhyme.

I get three thousand and expenses
a car, vouchers,
but I'm an accountant.

They do what I tell them,
my company.
What do *you* do?

Nasty little words, nasty long words,
it's unhealthy.
I want to wash when I meet a poet.

They're Reds, addicts,
all delinquents.
What they write is rot.

Mr Hines says so, and he's a schoolteacher,
he ought to know.
Go and find *work*.

Basil Bunting

For Adult Eyes Only: Strictly Private

Nine rhymes out of ten, poems are handed down by mothers. And as a child I loved them: poems that you could smell and taste; poems that came alive and ate you up; poems, light and mischievous as balloons. Nursery rhymes and fairy tales, strong in rhythm and image, were as much a part of my early childhood as bibs and pobs.

At the age of five, when I started school and became an Infant, things changed but not unduly. I learned to sing and chant aloud with others. The poems became longer, but as there were more of us anyway, that seemed to even things out. Street rhymes and playground songs were added to the armoury of charms and spells that I'd picked up to entice people or scare them away. There were prayers, of course. Hymns and litanies, often in Latin, became my private mantras.

After ten or eleven, the poetry disappeared. I don't know where it went but it came back with a painful bang three or four years later. Great chunks of Palgrave's *Golden Treasury* were heaved at me and my classmates by teachers – because they were paid to and because the syllabus demanded it. The poems seemed heavy and dusty, old-fashioned and outside my emotional range. At the time I don't think any of us could name one living poet.

Not unreasonably, I failed 'O' level Eng. Lit. which meant I didn't get to dissecting and unappreciating more poems at university, and although I regretted not continuing English, in retrospect it was perhaps a blessing in disguise. For as a poet I was free to write without the Ghost of Critics Past peering over my shoulder.

For in my late teens and early twenties I felt a strong need to express myself, to communicate. I was the outsider, the seer, the shaman, I was a duck who thought he'd invented water. I tried music first, then painting and then I began to listen to the rhythms inside my head and the poetry began.

I am on the side therefore of the ninety-nine per cent of kids who do not come top in English, and I have set out to provide a collection of poems that will speak to them. On the assumption that it's easier to make contact with poems that use a recognizably contemporary voice, I've gone for poets that are for the most part alive and British. Not every poem will make its mark with every reader, of course – no editor could hope for that. But I'd like to think that for every reader there will be two or three poems which strike home, and that the collection as a whole might recapture an interest that seemed to have been lost.

In making the selection I have confined my sources to the books and magazines that have gravitated towards me over the years. The result is a collection of poems that mean something – many different things – to me and which I believe could appeal to a young reader.

Inevitably there are some fine poets whose work I have omitted (R. S. Thomas, Charles Tomlinson, Geoffrey Hill, etc.) but only because I believe their work would be too difficult for most young readers. This does not imply that the poems are in any way

simple or unsophisticated, but they are, I believe,
accessible, and their light shines through more easily.
I wish to thank Clare Manifold, Carol Ann Duffy and
Tony Lacey for helping me to produce this anthology.
My thanks also to the poets.

Roger McGough

I cannot give the reasons
I only sing the tunes
The sadness of the seasons
The madness of the moons

Mervyn Peake

Index of First Lines

His case is typical. 30
hurt results away 90

I 92
I am waiting for you. 41
I come from Salem County 152
I desire that my body be 76
I hear that since you left me 124
I'll stand the lot of you, I said 154
I'm a left wing radish, raw and 26
I'm big for ten years old 26
I'm 11. And I don't really know 19
I remember, on a long 150
I remember once being shown the black bull 136
I said, 112
I saw a jolly hunter 141
I spend my days 147
'I usth thu workth in the thircusth,' 157
I visited the place where we last met. 123
I wandered lonely as 98
I wanted your soft verges 109
I watch you watching her. 111
I wish that woman in the 114
If 89
In Leyton the blizzards 93
In Manchester there are a thousand puddles. 168
In Tombstone there was, it seems, 149
It's a long time since I saw 137
It's true I knew her Mother burned; 55

John Wayne died of it 166
Just you look at me, man, 25

Love is feeling cold in the back of vans 108
Lovers lie around in it. 164
Lying apart now, each in a separate bed, 72
Lying awake, in the room 73

Many policemen wear upon their shoulders 157
Moving through the garden, brooding, trowel held like 65
My Aunty Jean 63
My father's temper was as hot 74

Index of Authors

Acknowledgements

The editor and publishers gratefully acknowledge permission to reproduce copyright poems in this book.
JOHN ASHBROOK: By permission of the author. MARGARET ATWOOD: Reprinted from *Power Poticits* by permission of the author. VERITY BARGATE: By permission of the author. WILLIAM BEDFORD: By permission of the author. PATRICIA BEER: By permission of the author. OLGA BENJAMIN: By permission of the author. PETE BROWN: By permission of the author. ALAN BROWNJOHN: Reprinted from *Sandgrains on a Tray*, Macmillan Ltd, by permission of the author. BASIL BUNTING: Reprinted from *Collected Poems* © Basil Bunting 1978, by permission of Oxford University Press. JIM BURNS: Reprinted from *A Simple Flower* by permission of Andium Press Ltd. DAVE CALDER: 'Strangers and Sweets' © 1972 reprinted from *Dealers and Dancers*, Raven Books, by permission of the author; 'Cabbages' © 1979 reprinted from *Batik*, Toulouse Press, by permission of the author. CHARLES CAUSLEY: Reprinted from *Collected Poems*, by permission of the author and Macmillan Ltd. TONY CONNOR: By permission of the author. BETH CROSS: By permission of the author. IVOR CUTLER: 'Alone' and 'What?' from *A Flat Man*, reprinted by permission of Trigram Press, © Ivor Cutler 1977. KIM DAMMERS: 'MANIC depressant' first published by Gallery Series Three/Poets, Harper Square Press, c/o Artcrest Products Co. Inc., Chicago, Illinois, USA. PETER DIXON: by permission of the author. CAROL ANN DUFFY: By permission of the author. GAVIN EWART: 'Arithmetic' from *The Deceptive Grin of the Gravel Porters*, London Magazine Editions, reprinted by permission of the author; 'Yorkshiremen in Pub Gardens' from *No Fool Like an Old Fool*, Gollancz Ltd, reprinted by permission of the author. PETER FALLON: Reprinted from *The Speaking Stones* by permission of the author. VICKI FEAVER: By permission of the author; 'Slow Reader', first published in *The Times Literary Supplement*. RAYMOND GARLICK: Reprinted from *Incense*, Gwasg Gomer, Llandysul, 1976, by permission of the author. MILES GIBSON: Reprinted from *The Guilty Bystander* by permission of the author and Methuen & Co. Ltd. HENRY GRAHAM: 'Nebula' by permission of the author; 'Sociosexual Primer for Children' reprinted from *Good Luck to you, Kafka, you'll need it Boss*, 1969, by permission of the author and André Deutsch Ltd. MARTIN HALL: By permission of the author. SPIKE HAWKINS: By permission of the author. SEAMUS HEANEY: Reprinted from *Wintering Out* by permission of Faber and Faber Ltd. ADRIAN HENRI· 'Love is ...' reprinted from *Penguin*

Glasgow to Saturn; 'Sir Henry Morgan's Song' from *The New Divan* reprinted by permission of the author and Carcanet New Press. GARETH OWEN: 'Winter', 'Time Child' and 'Unemployable' from *Salford Road* by Gareth Owen, Kestrel Books, 1979, © 1976, 1979 by Gareth Owen, reprinted by permission of Penguin Books Ltd. 'Street Boy' © 1974 by Gareth Owen, from *Salford Road*, Kestrel Books, 1979, reprinted by permission of Deborah Rogers Ltd, London. ALASDAIR PATERSON: By permission of the author. BRIAN PATTEN: 'Somewhere between Heaven and Woolworths' from *Little Johnny's Confession* and 'A Blade of Grass', 'Sometimes it Happens' from *Vanishing Trick* reprinted by permission of the author and George Allen & Unwin (Publishers) Ltd. TOM PICKARD: Reprinted from *Hero Dust*, Allison and Busby Ltd, and *Guttersnipe*, City Lights, USA, by permission of the author. TOM RAWORTH: By permission of the author. VERNON SCANNELL: 'Uncle Edward's Affliction', 'A Case of Murder' by permission of Allison and Busby Ltd, and 'Spy Story' by permission of the Poetry Society. JAMES SIMMONS: By permission of the author. ANNE STEVENSON: By permission of the author. SUSAN TAYLOR: By permission of the author. JOHN O. THOMPSON: By permission of the author. GAEL TURNBULL: By permission of the author. MARTIN WARD: By permission of the author. KIT WRIGHT: 'My Version' and 'Every Day in Every Way' by permission of the author; 'Sergeant Brown's Parrot' from *Rabbiting On* reprinted by permission of the author and Fontana Lions.

Every effort has been made to trace copyright holders, but in a few cases this has proved impossible. The editor and publishers apologize for these unwilling cases of copyright transgression and would like to hear from any copyright holders not acknowledged.

Also by Roger McGough in Plus

IN TIME OF WAR

This is a stunning collection of poetry that takes you right to the heart of the world at war   a world of bombs, blackouts and broken relationships, of patriotism, propaganda and unforgettable pain. There are poems from both First and Second World Wars, including work by Siegfried Sassoon, Rose Macaulay, Wilfred Gibson, A. A. Milne, Vera Brittain and Spike Milligan.

SO FAR, SO GOOD

Here, in this sharp and vivid collection of poetry, is all the fun. frustration, the love, hope and despair of teenage life, and all its unforgettable characters and experiences. A book to speak to all teenagers.

YOU TELL ME

Roger McGough and Michael Rosen

A collection of largely humorous poems by these two well-known poets. Sad, funny, serious and zany, they focus thoughtfully on everday life.

A BOOK OF MILLIGANIMALS
SILLY VERSE FOR KIDS
UNSPUN SOCKS FROM A CHICKEN'S LAUNDRY

Spike Milligan

Lunatic verse, which works like a dream.

WOULDN'T YOU LIKE TO KNOW

Michael Rosen

A collection of forty poems, including several specially written for this Puffin edition. Michael Rosen has a regular children's poetry column in the *Sunday Times* Colour Magazine.

SONGS FOR MY DOG AND OTHER PEOPLE

Max Fatchen

A greatly entertaining, totally unpompous collection of funny poems, including many Raddled Riddles and Nutty Nursery Rhymes.

QUICK, LET'S GET OUT OF HERE!
Michael Rosen and Quentin Blake

A collection of poems about humorous, odd and real situations.

THE PUFFIN BOOK OF FUNNY VERSE
ed. Julie Watson

A variety of poems from favourite and contemporary poets as well as some lesser-known but eccentric and downright funny poems. A book which will captivate children and parents alike.

HOT DOG AND OTHER POEMS
Kit Wright

With cartoonist Posy Simmonds, Kit Wright has produced a book of poems that are really mustard.

POEMS FOR OVER 10-YEAR-OLDS
ed. Kit Wright

Old and modern, familiar and unknown are all brought together in this book, suitable for children, their parents and their teachers.

LOCKED IN TIME
Lois Duncan

When seventeen-year-old Nore arrives at the old Louisiana plantation home of her father and his new wife, she is prepared for unhappiness. She did not expect her new family to be so different, nor can she understand her own mixed-up feelings about them. Her new mother is exotically beautiful, yet Nore senses evil . . .

KILL-A-LOUSE WEEK AND OTHER STORIES
Susan Gregory

The new head arrives at Davenport Secondary just at the beginning of the 'Kill-a-Louse' campaign. Soon the whole school is in uproar . . .

BASKETBALL GAME
Julius Lester

Allen is black and Rebecca is white, and in Nashville, Tennessee, in 1956 that means they must keep apart. They're interest in each other, but is that enough to survive the deeply rooted prejudice that surrounds them?

THE TRICKSTERS
Margaret Mahy

The Hamiltons gather at their holiday house for their custom-
ary celebration of midsummer Christmas in New Zealand but
it is to be a Christmas they'll never forget. For the warm,
chaotic family atmosphere is chilled by the unexpected arrival
of three sinister brothers – the Tricksters.

AT THE SIGN OF THE DOG AND ROCKET
Jan Mark

When her father slips a disc, school-leaver Lilian Goodwin
realizes she's in for a frantic couple of weeks in charge of the
family's pub – and the last thing she needs is a rude and
condescending temporary bar help like Tom to train.

BREAKING GLASS
Brian Morse

When the Red Army drops its germ bomb on Leicester, the
affected zone is sealed off permanently – with Darren and his
sister Sally inside it. Immune to the disease which kills Sally,
Darren must face alone the incomprehensible hatred of two of
the few survivors trapped with him. And the haunting ques-
tion is: why did Dad betray them?